HATFIELD
AND ITS PEOPLE

THE STORY OF A NEW TOWN, A GARDEN CITY,
AN OLD VILLAGE, A HISTORIC HOUSE, THE
FARMS AND THE COUNTRYSIDE
IN A HERTFORDSHIRE PARISH

discovered and related by
the
HATFIELD W.E.A.

(Members of the Hatfield Local History Tutorial Class of
Cambridge University Extra-Mural Board, organized by the
Hatfield Branch of the Workers' Educational Association, under
the tutorship of
Lionel M. Munby, M.A.)

PART 11B

FAMILIES AND TRADES
(Second Part, pages 49-99)

First published, July 1964
Published with index, April 2014

First published by the Hatfield Branch of the
Workers' Educational Association 1964

Published with index by Hatfield Local History Society 2014

Printed on demand via www.lulu.com

Original text by Henry W. Gray
Line drawings by Henry W. Gray
Photographs by Henry W. Gray and others
Index by Hazel K. Bell
Cover design by Henry W. Gray

This reprint was prepared by members of Hatfield Local History Society
with the kind permission of the Workers' Educational Association.

ISBN 978-0-9928416-1-4

COVER DESIGN

Top: D.H.82A Tiger Moth, one of the first aircraft to be built at
        Hatfield

Bottom: Nos. 16-22 Park Street. The centre house occupies the
        site of the "Holly Bush", the Walbys' original butcher's
        shop.

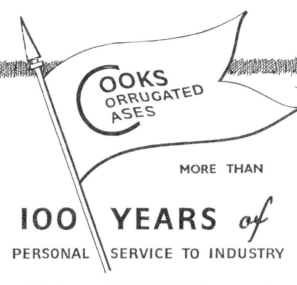

JOHN MOWLEM

and Company Limited

Builders and Civil Engineering Contractors

Head Office **91 Ebury Bridge Road London S.W.1**

Telephone SLOane 4500

Telegrams Mowlem - London - Telex

Also at **Edinburgh**
Cambridge
Doncaster
East Africa
Hong Kong
Yugoslavia
Malaysia
British Guiana

HERTFORDSHIRE LOCAL HISTORY COUNCIL

President: The Most Hon. The Marquess of Salisbury, K.G., P.C., F.S.A.

Publications:

HERTFORDSHIRE PAST & PRESENT (annually); free to members, 3/6 to the public.

COUNTY BIBLIOGRAPHY Part II: Periodicals and Transactions relating to Hertfordshire. M. F. Thwaite, 1959, 12/6.

DOMESDAY TABLES FOR THE COUNTY OF HERTFORD: Reprinted from Baring's Domesday Tables 1909; 1961, 2/6.

HERTFORDSHIRE POPULATION STATISTICS 1563—1801, Lionel Munby, 1964, 6/- to members, 7/6 to the public.

POTTERS AND KILNS IN MEDIEVAL HERTFORDSHIRE. Derek F. Renn, 1964, 3/6 to members, 4/- to the public.

Obtainable from: THE HON. EDITOR, MUSEUM, PAYNES PARK, HITCHIN

Membership of the Council is open to all interested persons. The subscription is 10/- a year. Details from the Hon. Secretary, 2 Vigors Croft, Hatfield.

FOREWORD

WHEN this series of booklets was published 50 years ago, it was rightly regarded as an exceptionally authoritative and informative work. It has since remained unchallenged as the prime source of reference for anyone interested in the history of Hatfield. Recognising its enduring value, members of Hatfield Local History Society have undertaken this reissue.

Since the booklets first appeared, some of the information contained in them has inevitably become out of date. Hatfield has been affected by sweeping changes, not least by the departure of the aircraft industry and the establishment in its place of a flourishing university and business park. Nevertheless, the original series has stood the test of time remarkably well. We know from our own research experience that it remains immensely useful and we have decided against attempting any piecemeal revision. Instead we have thought it better to reproduce the original booklets without making any changes, except for correcting obviously unintended typographical errors. An important difference is that much more comprehensive indexes have been added.

We hope that the reappearance of the work will stimulate others to undertake new research into Hatfield's more recent past.

Amongst the team who have undertaken the reissue is Henry W. Gray, M.V.O., one of the authors who took part in the W.E.A. class, led by the late Lionel Munby, which produced the original series. The others are Christine Martindale and Jane Teather, Chairman and Publications Officer respectively of Hatfield Local History Society, Hazel K. Bell, who created the new comprehensive indexes, Robin Harcourt Williams, formerly Librarian and Archivist to the Marquess of Salisbury, and G. Philip Marris who led the project.

Thanks are due to Mill Green Museum for allowing some of the original photographs to be re-scanned.

The *Workers' Educational Association,* founded in 1903, is a charity and the UK's largest voluntary sector provider of adult education, delivering 9,500 part-time courses for over 74,000 people each year in England and Scotland.

Hatfield Local History Society is an association of people interested in the history of Hatfield. The Society's aims and objectives are to encourage and undertake research into Hatfield's history, to produce publications and to provide a forum for the exchange of information on the history of the Hatfield area.

The Society is grateful to the copyright owners, the Hatfield Branch of the Workers' Educational Association, for permission to reissue the *Hatfield and its People* series. The complete list of titles is as follows:

Part 1	A Thousand Years of History
Part 2	The Story of Roe Green and South Hatfield
Part 3	Pubs and Publicans
Part 4	Newgate Street
Part 5	Roads and Railways
Part 6	Law and Disorder
Part 7	Churches
Part 8	Schools
Part 9	Farming Yesterday and Today
Part 10	Houses
Part 11A	Families and Trades (Part A)
Part 11B	Families and Trades (Part B)
Part 12	The Twentieth Century.

Please contact Hatfield Local History Society for further information about this publication.

INTRODUCTION

ALTHOUGH from Tudor times, and before, Hatfield has been the home of many influential families of county and national importance, these pages are not concerned with them. Rather are they an attempt to tell the story of some local families who, though not recorded in county or national histories, nevertheless contributed to the growth of the Hatfield we know today.

It is obviously only possible to mention but a minute fraction of those, who over the centuries have made up the parish of Hatfield. In this booklet will be found something of some families of the past, some present-day families who remained faithful to the parish of their ancestors, some past craftsmen, and something about those who have looked after the bodily health of the community.

My interest in the families that make up the Hatfield of today and of past centuries originated in tracing my own family's connection with the parish through some six or seven generations, and much of the information in this and the previous booklet is based on a collection of pedigrees of local families that I have assembled over the past decade.

As well as (and also forming part of) these pedigrees, the chief sources used in compiling Parts 11a and 11b of this Series, were as follows:

At Hatfield House:

> Transcripts of Hatfield Manor Court Rolls and Manor Papers, by R. T. Gunton.
> Various original deeds.

At Hatfield Parish Church:

> Parish Registers.
> Map of Hatfield Parish, 1824.

At the County Record Office, Hertford:

> Wills and Administrations (Archdeaconry of Huntingdon).
> Probate Inventories.
> Parish Registers and Bishops' Transcripts of Parish Registers.
> Allen's Marriage Index.
> Tithe-map and Schedule, 1838.
> Land Tax Returns.
> Rate Books.
> Window Tax Returns.
> Militia Returns.
> Court Rolls of the Manor of Astwick.
> Miscellaneous deeds, sale catalogues and other papers.
> County newspapers.

At the Public Record Office:

> Census Returns, 1841 and 1851.
> Hearth Tax Return, 1663.

At Somerset House:
  Wills and Administrations (Prerogative Court of Canterbury).

At St. Albans City Library:
  Trade Directories.
  Local newspapers.

At Guildhall Library, London:
  "The British Universal Directory," 1794.

A copy of map and schedule of Hatfield Town in 1838.

"Gentleman's Magazine," 18th-19th centuries.
The standard County Histories of Hertfordshire.
"John Briant," by H. C. Andrews, 1930.
"From Chindwin to Criccieth," by Charles Drage, 1956.
"The History of Paper Mills in Hertfordshire" by E. T. Finerty, in
    "The Paper-Maker," April, May, June, 1957.

I am indebted to the Marquess of Salisbury for access to material at Hatfield House, and am most grateful to Miss Clare Talbot for the time and trouble she has taken in making these documents available. My thanks are due to past and present Rectors of Hatfield for access to the parish registers, and to the Staff of the County Record Office. I also wish to acknowledge the help and advice of Mr. F. Bradbeer, Mrs. G. M. Brown, Mr. R. L. Drage, Miss L. D. Gray, Dr. and Mrs. Kenneth Hutton, Mr. Gerald Millington, Mr. Lionel Munby, Mr. J. Naden, Mr. R. C. Simmons, and many other friends and relatives.

It was inferred in Book 11a, p. 36, that the Palmer family, descendants of old John Palmer the centenarian, no longer lived in the town. My apologies are due to the several members of this old family who do indeed continue to live in the neighbourhood, and who, besides this interesting relationship, can also claim descent through the Lambs, from the 17th century Hare family, and through the Kentishes, from the early 17th century yeoman Smiths of Roe Green.

                                                                    H.W.G.

Migration into Hatfield

THROUGHOUT Hatfield's history, change has taken place but slowly, and as has been seen in the last booklet, the sense of stability and continuity has been strong. Though many of the families who made up the community may have stayed only one or two generations before moving on to a neighbouring parish or to the City, at any one time a good percentage would have been found to be Hertfordshire born and bred (in 1851 eighty per cent, of the Town population).

Over the years, however, there have been periods when fresh blood has come to the Town from further afield. Just as the last decade has seen a great influx of Londoners, so last century, to a lesser extent, Hatfield became the home of a number of Scottish farming families (see Book 9, p. 34) and smallholders from South Bedfordshire. Another noticeable influx of "foreigners" occurred in the 16th century—this time from the West. This last migration, though apparently fairly general throughout the country, due to the advent of the Welsh Tudors to the English throne, was no doubt increased in Hatfield by the town's close association with the later Tudor sovereigns, and with not a few of their Court officials, who brought with them their family servants and retainers. Certainly by the time the series of Bishops' transcripts (of the parish registers) begin in 1604, a number of Welsh families were living in the parish: such names as Davies, Evans, Hughs (Hews), ap John, Jones, Leweis, Lloyd (Fludde), Morgan, Phillips, Price and Vaughan occurring in the period to 1620. Perhaps some of these families had come in the train of the Onslows. Fulk Onslow, a native of Salop, had obtained the lease of Hatfield Rectory in 1560, and resided at the Parsonage House till his death in 1602 (see Book 7, pp. 5 and 10). Certainly one of Onslow's servants was William Edwardes alias William ap Rutherche ap Edwarde, who died at Hatfield in the 1590's, and who willed "that some money and other things be bestowed for remembrance upon my fellow servants and other acquaintance pertaining towards my master his house." To his cousin Cadwallader Tidder, Edwardes left, "in recompence of his travayle and charges bestowed on me", forty shillings, together with his best hat, best doublet and best pair of hose.

Both Cadwallader Tidder (Tydder or Tudor) and his brother Thomas were also in the service of the Onslows at Hatfield. Indeed it was Cadwallader Tydder whom Parliament allowed to execute Fulk Onslow's duties of office as Clerk of the Parliaments when he was stricken with ague "until it shall please God to restore him to health."

Onslow, in his will, rewarded the Tydders, as he did his other servants, with generous legacies of money and property in Hatfield. In return Thomas Tydder remembered his patron and benefactor in the names of two of his children: Fulk (he entered the Church, and became Rector of Tewin and Stevenage), and Onslow Tydder. Meanwhile Thomas's brother, Cadwallader, appears to have followed his late master's relatives to Huntingdonshire, where, "being old and weak in body", he died in 1629. By his will he left legacies to various friends and relations, including ten groats apiece to six of his old mistress's servants living at Hatfield. A rather nice, human touch, comes towards the end of the will, when the old man appoints his brother Thomas Tydder, executor, desiring him "to remember my poore kindred at Hatfield whose names I have now forgott".

Some Old Hatfield Families

In spite of the most recent influx of newcomers to Hatfield there yet remains a good proportion of families whose ancestors are to be found enumerated in the census returns of a century and more ago. Such names as Angell, Austin, Beach, Bligh, Bracey, Burgess and Butterfield, Canham, Collarbone, Dunham, Elliott, Ewington and Flitney, Gillians, Gray, Gregory, Grovestock, Greenham, Groom, Hankin, Hart, Hickson, Hill, Hipgrave, Hulks and Lawrence, Mardell, Mardling, Moore and Munday, Naden, Nash, Pales, Palmer, Parrott, Payne, Powell, and Pratchett, Rumney, Sibley, Staines, Starkey, Streader, Thomas Tingey and Tyler, Valentine and Venables, Walby, Waters, Webster, Willson and Wren being readily recognisable. Some of these families were even then already well-established, for instance, the Collarbones had first settled here in 1666, the Greenhams in the 1680's, and the Moore family have lived in the parish since the 1650's. Other families are mentioned elsewhere in these booklets. But of the ordinary families of present day Hatfield perhaps two of the most interesting are those of Bassil and Currell.

CURRELL

In 1616 Christopher Corrall of Ayot St. Lawrence, who described himself as a labourer, left in his will legacies totalling five pounds. Among the beneficiaries were the two young children of his brother Richard, who lived not far away, at Cromer Hyde, in Hatfield. This Richard left numerous descendants (many of whom bore the Christian name of their 17th century progenitor) and was with little doubt ancestor of the Currells now living in the town.

During the 17th and early 18th centuries Richard and his progeny were yeoman farmers in the Cromer Hyde district and in North Mymms. In 1733 Richard Currell of North Mymms sold five cottages— later to become the site of the Market House—in Fore Street (Book 11a, p. 24). About thirty years later Richard's son sold the family's original holding at Cromer Hyde to Lord Melbourne, who at this time appears to have been consolidating his estate around Brocket Hall, in a similar manner to Lord Salisbury around Hatfield House (Book 11a, p. 40).

While after these sales, the fortunes of the local Currells seem to have gradually declined, their kinsmen were prospering in the City. Here Christopher Corrall, a Citizen and Goldsmith of London, was a successful gold and silver laceman. In 1787 he became Prime Warden of the Goldsmiths' Company and for twenty years he was one of the Common Council (the governing body) of the City of London. Dying in 1790, he was buried, as was his wish, "in the family vault at Hatfield, in decent but not expensive manner." His shop in Lombard Street he left to his eldest son Edward, who was probably the "Mr. Edward Corrall" from London, who was buried at Hatfield in 1828. Thus, although they had prospered in the City, the family obviously retained an affection for their ancestral parish.

In the year that Christopher Corrall the laceman died, one of his kinsmen, John Corrall, a journeyman papermaker, was one of the eleven men who were indicted for threatening to strike if their wages were not increased by a shilling a week (see p. 70, and Book 6, p. 17). Poor John, married that same year, died only two years later, in 1792. His cousins however, continued to live in the district, and in the 1851 census no fewer than eight households of Currells are enumerated—old Richard, aged 74, was a pauper and former hurdle-maker living at Dognell Green (ten years earlier he had been described as a farmer); the others were mostly agricultural labourers.

BASSILL

The Basill family, neighbours of the Currells in present day Hatfield as they were in 17th century Cromer Hyde, have lived in the parish (with but one short break) continuously since the days of Elizabeth I. Now the surname Basill, or Bassill as it was more often written, is a derivative of the name Bassilly or Baseley, a name that is found in Hatfield Court Rolls and grants from the 13th to the 15th centuries. If the 16th century Bassills could be proved to be descendants of this earlier family, then this would give an ordinary family living in the town today a direct male ancestry stretching back some 700 years in the same parish, a rare distinction indeed.

The connected pedigree of the Bassills, and the subsequent rise and fall of the family fortunes can however be traced back with certainty to 1587 (fig. 17) when the marriage of Symon Bassill, a yeoman, and Agnes Carnbrook took place at St. Stephen's Church, St. Albans. These were unsettled times, with the constant threat of invasion by Spain; only two years before Bassill's wedding, his neighbour, Sir John Brocket, had been in charge of mustering soldiers in this part of the county, and Bassill may have watched as the soldiery trained on nearby Nomansland Common, and as they marched off on their way to Tilbury Camp. And the year after their marriage Symon and his young wife no doubt shared in the general relief and the celebrations that followed the Armada's defeat.

Twelve years after his marriage Symon inherited certain lands and houses at Cromer Hyde from his kinsman, William Hill. The Hills themselves had owned the property for a considerable time, and it seems probable that William was a near relative of the Nicholas Hill who in

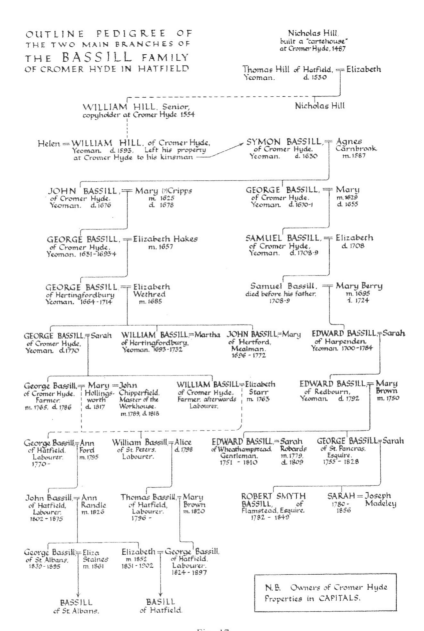

OUTLINE PEDIGREE OF
THE TWO MAIN BRANCHES OF
THE BASSILL FAMILY
OF CROMER HYDE IN HATFIELD

N.B. Owners of Cromer Hyde Properties in CAPITALS.

Fig. 17.

56

1487 had been presented at the Manor Court for building a house called a 'Cartehouse' on the King's highway at Cromer Hyde, and four years earlier had had the misfortune accidentally to kill his daughter while out ploughing (Book 6, p. 7).

Symon Bassill, who held with two others the lease of the tithes of corn, hay and hops, etc., of the Parsonage for £320, was undoubtedly a man of some note in the parish, and in 1615 he held the responsible office of churchwarden here (as also did George Bassill in 1660). In 1606 he (with his wife and children) inherited most of his father-in-law's property; Bassill's three servants were not forgotten either—they received sixpence each from Carnbrook's will. By the time Symon died in 1630 he must have been a comparatively old man, and had probably already handed over part of his farm to his two sons. The inventory made after his death, shows he must have lived a plain, straightforward life, with not much luxury.

Symon's younger son, George, continued to farm at Cromer Hyde till his own death forty years after his father. The sense of the close-knit community of the 17th century was very marked, and just as his father's inventory had been appraised by (amongst others) his neighbour Richard Currell, this same duty was performed after George's death by Richard's son, Nicholas Currell. The value of George's goods and stock was put at £157 17s. 0d.—almost twice that of his father's. From George were descended the Bassills who later farmed at Harpenden, Wheathampstead, Redbourn, Flamstead and district, the senior line of which continued to own an estate of 48 acres at Cromer Hyde until at least 1856 (fig. 17). This line evidently prospered; by the late 18th century Edward Bassill of Wheathampstead had risen to the ranks of the gentry, while his younger brother, George, and nephew Robert Smyth Bassill, were described in the "Gentleman's Magazine" when they died, as "Esquire," and when the latter made his will in 1848, he was in a position to leave monetary legacies totalling £4,300 (including £500 to the treasurer and trustees of the West Herts Infirmary, at Hemel Hempstead). Further, when Robert's sister, Mrs. Sarah Madeley, the last Bassill to own the Cromer Hyde property, died in 1856, she left legacies amounting to over £15,700.

Meanwhile the elder branch of old Symon's family, who remained at Cromer Hyde, added to their possessions by the inheritance by George Bassill on his twenty-first birthday (1652) of "the howse called Hornebeame Hall wherein one Nicholas Ivory now dwelleth in, with twoe closes", which had been left him by (?his grandfather) Thomas Cripps, yeoman. Five years later George was married, at St. Albans Abbey. His son moved to Hertingfordbury, where he farmed Place Farm, and was chosen chief constable of the Hundred in 1701. Of *his* three surviving sons, the second remained at Hertingfordbury, the youngest became a prosperous meal-merchant at Hertford, while the eldest son George, returned to Cromer Hyde, where he continued to farm the Bassill lands.

57

Following George's death in 1770, the original farm of old Symon Bassill was sold to the local landowner, Lord Melbourne. From a Brocket Park estate map of 1798 we see that a farm of about 50 acres then enclosed in Brocket Park (the site of the present Warren Farm and plantation) between the river and the Wheathampstead road at Cromer Hyde, included a field named Bassills Field, and this 50 acres probably represents the original Bassill and Hill holding. It seems, however, that after the sale George's elder son and namesake continued to work the old family lands as tenant of Lord Melbourne. While the elder son had received part of the proceeds from the sale of this farm, the younger son, William, had been left Hornbeam Hall, which in the 1750's had been licensed as an alehouse known as the "Chequers" (Book 3, pp. 20-21 and fig. 10). After mortgaging it in 1776, four years later William sold the property to Searancke's Brewery, although he too appears to have remained at his old home, as tenant. After these sales —while the junior line of the family, as has been seen, were prospering at Harpenden and Redbourn — the fortunes of this, the elder branch, declined, and the next generation are found in marked contrast, as labourers.

This reversal in the family fortunes was not helped by the fact that William had brought into the world no less than twelve children, most, if not all, of whom survived. It perhaps also explains a note amongst the Archdeaconry papers of 1784 regarding William Bassill of Cromer Hyde, who was two years in arrears with his church rates!

Both George and his brother William had sons named George (both born in 1770) and William, which creates something of a problem of identities in the next generation. However, what is certain is that the family, although now landless, did not move far from their ancestral home. In 1841 William Bassill, an agricultural labourer, was living at Winches Farm, Smallford, while his cousins William and Frederick, also agricultural labourers were at Lemsford, and John Bassill, in 1841 living at Ellenbrook, was ten years later one of the original inhabitants of the first Hatfield New Town. In 1852 John's daughter married her cousin George Bassill, and from this marriage are descended the Basills and their kin living in Hatfield today.

FEMALE DESCENTS

The Basills and Currells represent the survival of local families in the male line. More difficult to trace is descent through female lines, which often represent even longer residence in a single parish. The outstanding example of this type of descent yet noticed in this parish is that of the Horn family, now represented by Mr. J. B. Horn of Welwyn Garden City. At first sight the family appears to be one of the many Bedfordshire immigrants of the first half of the 19th century, but on further investigation, it has been possible to trace the family's ancestors back on various sides (Book 11a, fig. 4) to the 18th century Coxes, the 17th century Tharps, Johnsons and Beasneys, and finally back to the Battell family of 15th century Hatfield.

A rental of Bedwell Manor in 1468 informs us that Robert Battell held a tenement and land at Wild Hill, and from the will of probably this same Robert, made in 1501, we can see the family at this period were of some consequence, owning property at Stanborough, Ludwickhyde, Holwellhyde, Buckhamwykhyde (Woodside) and Hatfield Thorpe (the Town), in addition to property in Essendon and Hertingfordbury. In February 1509-10 Humphrey Battell (son and heir of Robert), yeoman, of Hatfield, appears in the Patent Rolls as one of a number of people granted a general pardon by Henry VIII at the beginning of his reign. In 1548 Humphrey's son, William Battell of Stanborough, was himself in trouble at Hatfield Manor Court for having enclosed upon the Lady's (Princess Elizabeth's) lands lying in "Middlefeld at Hansyde."

Although the family moved to Digswell later in the century (Robert Battell's brass, 1557, is still to be seen in Digswell Church), and the next generation to Welwyn, they retained their Stanborough and Woodside property, and in the 17th century the three brothers, John, Affabel and Robert are found back at Hatfield. Affabel farmed Ludwickhyde, and through his son of the same name (who married Dionise Searancke) was ancestor of two Rectors of Digswell and a Sub-Dean of the Chapels Royal to Queen Anne. Meanwhile the third brother, Robert, and his descendants remained in the parish, farming at Stanborough, and the property they owned there (probably the site of the original "Bull" Inn) remained in the family well into the 18th century.

About 1699 William Battell of Stanborough purchased the eighty acres of Upper Handside Farm. With William's death in 1722-3 the male line of this branch of the family became extinct, and his property was inherited by his sister Mary. From her, Upper Handside came to William Tharp, husband of her niece Sarah (Book 11a, fig. 4). With Tharp's second marriage in 1732 to the Widow Johnson, and the union seventeen years later of his son William to his step-sister, the heiress Sarah Johnson, more property (in Hatfield Town and at Gosmore) came into the family. The younger William and Sarah Tharp, whose only son predeceased them, were survived by two daughters—Ann, wife of William Cox of Stanborough, and Sarah, wife of Edmund Fearnley of Bell Bar—between whom the considerable family estate was divided. The Coxes and Fearnleys further benefited in the 1820's from the wills of their distant cousins, the Whittingstalls, who had made a fortune as millers during the Napoleonic Wars. On his death in 1822 George Whittingstall had left an estate of nearly £700,000, and it was to Sarah Fearnley's son Edmund that he left his brewery at Watford, together with its public houses and £5,000 worth of stock-in-trade. Edmund added the surname of his benefactor to his own, and was ancestor of the well-known Fearnley-Whittingstall family.

The old Battell estate at Handside descended in the Fearnley-Whittingstall side of the family (until, following bankruptcy, it was sold in 1857 to Earl Cowper), and formed part of the lands farmed successfully throughout the 19th century, and indeed until the building of Welwyn Garden City, by various members of the Cox family and by the Horns.

In the mid-1830's William Cooper Horn, whose father had come from Bedfordshire to farm in Hertfordshire, became tenant of Earl Cowper at Lower Handside Farm, but died a young man four years after his marriage. The marriage of his only surviving son, William James Horn in 1860 to Sarah Cox, grand-daughter of the above William and Ann Cox, thus brought to the Horn family as ancestors many of Hatfield's most prominent yeoman families — families which had farmed in the Stanborough and Handside district for 350 years and more, and who had played their full part in the affairs of the parish for many generations. This tradition was to be carried on to the full by W. J. Horn himself, for apart from successfully farming most of the land on which the original Welwyn Garden City was built, he took a prominent part in local affairs; a J.P. and Chairman of the old Board of Guardians, he was chosen first Chairman of Hatfield R.D.C. in 1895; he was also a founder-member of the Hertfordshire County Council (1889), to which he was elected an Alderman, and for 57 years he served as a Churchwarden at Lemsford. This tradition was carried on also by his sons, one of whom, the late Mr. W. C. Horn, was last Chairman of Welwyn Garden City Parish Council, becoming first Chairman of the Urban District Council on its formation in 1927.

Some other well-established Farming Families

Perhaps one of the most widespread Hertfordshire families, whose name is to be found in most parishes in the county at one time or another, are the Biggs. From the 14th to the 19th century the family constantly finds its way into Hatfield records, as farmers, millers and brewers. In the lay subsidy collected in 1545, Richard, William and John Bigg appear, the latter contributing 20 shillings — the fourth largest assessment in the parish. At this date also Freeman Bigg was owner of considerable land, including Downs Farm, as well as the important "George" Inn, which last, following his death, was kept by his son William (Book 3, p. 10). In the latter 1500's Edward Bigg was tenant of Symondshyde Farm, while another branch of the family—William and his son Anthony—farmed at Ludwick Hall between 1565 and 1640. A John Bigg farmed in the Ludwickhyde district during the second half of the 17th century.

These farming Biggs seem to have died out or left the parish in the later 1600's, but another branch re-appears in 1726, when Joseph Bigg from Great Munden took the lease of Hatfield Mill at a rent of £55. By the agreement Bigg was allowed a year's rent for repairs, but was to pay for the mill stones and gears then in the mill which had belonged to the previous lessee, Joseph Huntman. The lease also contained the clause that Bigg was not to take from the river any trout, eels or other fish.

It can be assumed the Biggs prospered as millers, for when Joseph died in 1767 he was able to leave £1,600 to his three grandchildren. Four generations of the family held the mill until about 1824, when the last Joseph Bigg gave up the trade, having, it is said, gambled away some £20,000 of the family property. It was the last Joseph's sister, Mary Bigg, who married in 1832 Mark Powell, a papermaker, who afterwards set up business in Fore Street (p. 70 and Book 11a, p. 22).

When the Biggs left Hatfield Mill in the 1820's, the lease was acquired by another well-known Hertfordshire farming and milling family—the Farrs. They already held Withy Mill (rebuilt after a fire, about 1830 and re-named Cecil Mill), having first come to the parish from Kimpton in the late 18th century. The Farr family remained Hatfield's millers until the death of old George Farr in 1884. During the 19th century they were among the leading farmers in the parish, the family between them, as well as holding the mills, farming a considerable part of the Hatfield Hyde area (Woodhall Lodge, Peartree, Leggs, etc.).

The last of the Farrs of Woodhall Lodge left an only daughter who married John Hammond White, whose sons continued the family farming tradition till recent years, at Roe Green, and at West End, Essendon.

The other great farming family of 19th century Hatfield was that of Webb. In 1811 William Webb had married one of the daughters of Edmund Simpkins, the butcher of Fore Street (Book 11a, p. 14). Eleven years later he obtained the lease of Birchwood Farm, and in 1827 acquired the licence of the "Red Lion" Inn, and farmed the land belonging to that. Throughout most of the remainder of the century various members of his family retained both the Inn and Birchwood, and also farmed Stanborough, Astwick Lodge and Barbers Lodge Farms. Between 1819 and 1882, with but one short break, three members of this family held office as churchwardens at Hatfield, William Webb, followed by his brother-in-law James Simkins, who was followed by William James Webb, son of the first William.

Contemporaries of the Webbs were the Nightingalls, farmers of a considerable amount of land in the first half of the 19th century. They were also the last landlords of the "Angell" Inn at Brickwall Hill, before it closed about 1850. The "Angell", being only a short distance from Brocket Park, was no doubt a convenient meeting place for the racing fraternity attending the fashionable annual races held in the Park during the Regency period. It seems more than likely that it was this that fostered the interest in horses and racing in the younger John Nightingall, and led him to leave the district in the 1860's for South Hatch, Epsom, where he set up as a horse trainer. At Epsom John was followed by several generations of successful trainers and jockeys, and the stables he founded are still, of course, in the hands of his descendant, the well-known trainer, Walter J. Nightingall.

Finally, though not a blood relationship, an interesting link with one of the best-known farming families of present day Hatfield can be traced back to a family of yeoman farmers who lived in the Hatfield and Essendon district in the 14th century. The Ludford family lived in the area from at least the 1300's until the mid-18th century, and a William de Ludeford was Rector of Essendon in 1346-7.

When the yeoman Henry Ludford died in 1670-1 his appraisers valued his effects—which included two Bibles, worth three shillings— at only £23 17s. 2d., but when his brother Nicholas died twelve years later, *his* goods were put at £450 18s. 0d. Nicholas Ludford was the farmer of Birchwood, and following his death the farm was carried on, at first by his eldest son, and later by his second son, Henry. But Henry died in 1689, only four years after his marriage, leaving a young family. His widow continued the lease, and soon afterwards appears to have married John Pratchett, who had the lease renewed in his own name in 1718. From then until 1822 Birchwood Farm remained in the hands of the younger branch of the Pratchett family. Charles Pratchett, grandson of John, one of the leading farmers in the district, was also for many years senior Churchwarden of the parish till his death in 1795, "Having lived in the Esteem and Respect of his Superiors and equals. A good Husband and Father and Master, A friendly Neighbour, Honestly industrious for the Interests of his Family and Lovingly attentive to those of the Poor" (— if we are to believe his epitaph). It was Charles's elder brother Leonard who kept the "Eight Bells" in 1769 (see Book 3, p. 23). Birchwood Farm was carried on by Charles's younger son, William, his elder son being, in the words of his will, "now, as I suppose, if alive, in the East Indies." On William's death in 1822 the Pratchett connection with Birchwood came to an end, although descendants of his many cousins (several of them builders and bricklayers) still live in the town.

It was William Pratchett's eldest daughter who married Francis Denyer Complin, the brewer and maltster of Park Street. One of the consequences of this marriage was that following Mrs. Complin's death her husband's cousin, Arthur James Sherriff came to Hatfield in 1872 to take over the lease of the Brewery, with its corn, coal and salt trade, and, of course, founded the well-known present day farming family (see also Book 3, p. 9, and Book 9, p. 9). With the greatly increased seed corn, fertilizers, feeding stuffs and potato trade, the coal business was dispensed with in 1950; by 1955 the family were farming about 2,000 acres in Hatfield and district, possibly even some of the same fields that were tilled by the Ludfords four- or five-hundred years earlier.

Potters, Brickmakers and Builders

The geological position of Hatfield has meant a plentiful supply of clay for pottery, tile and brick-making. Fragments of mediaeval pottery have been found near the site of known potteries in the parish, around Woodside. Bernard the potter is named in a survey of the Manor in 1251, and in 1396 five potters were granted a licence to dig clay in the Great Wood (see also Book 10, pp. 6-7).

The potter's trade, like other crafts, tended to run in families, and the wills of four 16th century Hatfield potters have survived—Henry Beane 1522, Richard Bene 1538, Henry Mannynge 1551 and Robert Mannynge 1571. A fifth, William Bateman, potmaker, by his will of 1617 left to his son John "my workynge wheele." Of little substance, his total inventory value was only £11 19s. 8d. In his "workeing house" his "wheele to worke upon wth certaine boardes used for his trade" was valued at 13s. 4d., while in the yard was "one little old carte" also worth 13s. 4d., in which he presumably took his pots to market. "One pigg, one gridlestone and a little hay, two henns and one cocke" in the yard were reckoned at 12s. 6d.

A pot kiln, in the 1700's and early 1800's owned by the Searanckes, remained in operation near the present "St. Michael's" at Woodside, till the death of Isaac Bryan, the last potter, in 1882. Fragments of the domestic ware (jugs, plates, etc.) made here, are still turned up in the field where the kiln stood.

Brickmaking on the other hand continued in Hatfield until thirty years ago, and until last century probably most of the bricks used in Hatfield were made locally. Three fairly ancient brickfields are known —a twenty-eight acre field between the Old Rectory, French Horn Lane, and the St. Albans Road, was described in a survey of the Parsonage of 1606-7 as "pasture ground called brickkill field"; Brickhill Close, alias Brickfield Close in 1611 was situated to the west of Ground Lane, and a third kiln was at Morrall Hill, on the far side of the Park. It was probably the latter which supplied the bricks for the building of Hatfield House between 1607 and 1611, and the huge pits from which the clay was dug can still be seen. None of the brickmakers named in the building accounts appear to have local names, so presumably they had been brought here specially. The prices charged for the bricks, it appears, were not always to the satisfaction of Lord Salisbury's steward, and the brickmakers George Collins and Thomas Yearly who charged 11s. 6d. per 1,000 were replaced by Ellis Elliott and Eustace Kelly—whose prices were more moderate, at 9s. 9d. per 1,000.

It is somewhat surprising not to find the name of Harrow among the building accounts, for this family appear to have been fairly prosperous bricklayers in the town at this time—and they continued in the same trade for a further two hundred years. The family had been in the parish, certainly since the late 1500's, and we hear of John

Harrow, a bricklayer, in 1613—just two years after the completion of the Great House. It was one of the Harrows, who with Thomas Avis, a carpenter, was given the job of converting the Great Hall of the Old Palace into stables in 1628, and indeed the stables remained in the Palace till the present century.

In the 1630's and '40's William Harrow was leasing from Lord Salisbury the Morrall Hill brickfield for the annual rent of 12,000 bricks, and in 1647 he was in trouble for having built a cottage on the field. A century later (1758) five of the parish's seven bricklayers eligible for militia service were members of the Harrow family, and their descendants continued the trade until the middle of last century.

In the mid-18th century one of the family who broke away from the trade was Andrew Harrow, publican of the "Eight Bells" in the 1750's. This period also produced another of the same family whose livelihood depended neither upon the victualling or bricklaying trades. This was the notorious William (Fudge) Harrow, who claimed he was the famous "flying highwayman," and whose gang terrorised the neighbourhood at this time. His downfall, which made headlines in the newspapers and journals of the period, was brought about following the robbery in 1762 of £300 from Thomas Glasscock, a local farmer. The gang made off, and Harrow himself got as far as Gloucestershire where he put up at an inn, posing as a deserter from a man-of-war. However, a quarrel arose between him and some drinking companions, and suspicion was aroused from Harrow always keeping loaded pistols near at hand, and from the large sum of money he had. Finding himself suspected he moved on to Worlibank in Staffordshire, where he was overtaken by his pursuers, who "found him in bed with his doxey" with three brace of pistols cocked and loaded on a chair beside the bed. Being taken by surprise before he could make use of his pistols, he put up no resistance, and was brought to trial at Hertford Assizes. Here, the following March, with his accomplices, Thomas Jones "the noted travelling ratcatcher," and William Bosford, he paid the final penalty for his numerous crimes, his execution being noted in the parish register of Hatfield.

Another brickmaking and bricklaying family of the 17th and 18th centuries was that of Chessum. In the 1680's Elizabeth Chessum held the lease of the Morrall Hill kiln, "with liberty to dig clay or sand anywhere within the field," for £10 per year. It was another of the same family—Andrew Chessum, brickmaker and limeburner—who did a deal in 1747-8 with Henry Calverly (or Caveller), who owned two cottages in Park street (No. 40), which had been allowed to "decay and become ruinous and uninhabitable." As Calverly could not afford to pay for their rebuilding, he contracted with Chessum to rebuild the two cottages, and in lieu of payment conveyed to Chessum one of the cottages so rebuilt.

In the 17th and 18th centuries Calverly's relations, the Johnsons, were themselves prosperous brickmakers—Henry Johnson, brickmaker and limeburner died in 1718 (Book 11a, fig. 4), and John Johnson his son, rented the Morrall Hill kiln in the 1730's. In the 1760's the brickfield and kiln was leased for £20 a year to James Bassill (who was also licensee of the "King's Head"), whose grandfather John Bassill—and through inference his father also—had been bricklayers earlier in the century.

During the second half of the 18th century the Morrall Hill kiln was in the hands of Benjamin Manfield, and as late as 1851 it appears to have been still working—William Lee, a brickmaker, and his two sons who were tilemakers, with Thomas Warren, a retired limeburner then living there.

Throughout the 19th century the Chapman family (Book 11a, fig. 11) were the town's leading bricklayers. The business had been started in the late 1700's by James Chapman, after whose death (1816), and that of his widow, it was carried on by their three sons in partnership. In 1851 James Chapman, builder, who lived at Priory House (fig. 18), was noted in the census as employing five men. The family appears to have done their own brickmaking and limeburning, their limekiln

Fig. 18. "Priory House," No. 50, Great North Road, 1960. Home of Joseph Bigg the brewer (Book 3, p. 7) in the early 1800's, and of the Chapman family, builders, for the rest of the century.

(*Photo: H. W. Gray*).

being situated in one of the Broomfields (now the site of Dellfield Road and Newtown School), which is still remembered by some as "Chapman's Field." The family name is still preserved in Chapman's Yard and Terrace, in Park Street, which were built and owned by the family in the middle of last century.

Other 19th century builders were James Webb of Newtown (his building included Newtown House—now demolished—and Flint Cottages (Book 10, fig. 1) in Newtown), and Benjamin Dunham.

At the turn of the century Josiah Smart was brickmaking, while in the 1920's the Baldock family (apparently earlier employed by Smart) had a brickfield and kiln near Manor Road, prior to the building of the By-Pass. The red bricks made here were used for building many of the cottages in Ground Lane and elsewhere in the vicinity. Later the Baldocks transferred their operations to the triangle of land between the present Burleigh School and the By-Pass, although the clay of this field was apparently somewhat inferior to that of the former site only a few yards away.

This brickworks closed down about 1930, at which time the business was in the hands of W. J. Richardson, a well-known local builder. "Jack" Richardson, who was once described as the most popular man in Hatfield, had been born in the town in 1861 (his father was a gardener on the Estate and his mother was a sister of Joseph Canham of the "Gun"—Book 3, p. 25). He learnt his craft in the carpenter's and joiner's shop on the Estate and later in London. In 1885 he set up on his own account as a builder, and from small beginnings soon became one of the most successful businessmen of the town, at one time employing over 100 men. His work included restorations of several old Hatfield houses (e.g. Morton House for F. W. Speaight), as well as work on the Old Palace, the oldest of Hatfield's brick buildings.

Clocks and Bells

The clockmaking business of William Burgess (1822-1890), a younger brother of James Burgess the bark-dealer of Batterdale (Book 11a, p. 39) and of his son, was well-known in Hatfield until sold in the 1920's, and many a Burgess timepiece is still in use. The town has in fact supported the clock and watch-making trade from at least the 18th century; part of the craftsman's work no doubt was to look after the clocks at the Great House.

In the early 1700's the inventory of Samuel Hare, the Batterdale maltster (died 1723), informs us that he possessed a clock which was kept in the parlour (at Batterdale House), but the whole of the furnishings of this room, including the clock, only amounted to £1 12s. 0d. probate value. His brother-in-law, however, the prosperous brewer, John Searancke, who died seven years earlier, had a much grander timepiece—his "clock and case" was valued at £3 0s. 0d. But even some of the more lowly folk had clocks in their homes, possibly family heirlooms: John Scare, alternatively described as a husbandman and a victualler, who died the same year as Samuel Hare, and whose total goods came to only £12 7s 6d., had "a clock upon ye stairhead" in his cottage.

Richard Endersbie (whose wife was buried in 1729) was described as a watchmaker, and was perhaps responsible for some of these instruments. In 1750 Thomas Uncle, watchmaker and shopkeeper, died, and the intricacies of his craft seem to be reflected in the precise instructions he left concerning his funeral: "And also my Will is that I may have a Shroud of 5 & 6, A Coffen of Eighteen Shillings; no Gloves &c: Only four men to carry me to Church at one Shilling each." Disappointingly, no inventory of his goods, which might have described his working tools, appears to have been made, or if it was then it has not survived.

Later in the century John Hinton carried on the trade here, and it was perhaps he who fostered the love for clocks and the like in the young John Briant (1749-1829) who later in life became widely known for his skill as a clockmaker and bellfounder. It was only while working on research for this booklet that it has come to light that the father of Briant (also named John) lived at Hatfield, and here presumably the young John spent part of his youth (having, it is said, been schooled at Newmarket). The elder Briant owned property here—the School House (now "Church Cottage") and two houses on the old London Road (near, or perhaps actually, "Lawn House")— which on his death he left to his only son. Whether the elder John had any interest in clockmaking is not known—when he made his will he called himself "Gentleman"—but it is intriguing that by his will he left to his son specifically "my three Boxes marked 1, 2, 3, and my Bureau and Books and my Chest of Tools." One wonders what kind of tools, and what was in the boxes marked 1, 2 and 3?

It may be that the elder Briant was in the service of the Earl of Salisbury, for as well as his Hatfield connection, at the time he made his will (1779) he was living at Clothall, near Baldock, where also lived the Earl of that day, at Quickswood House. When he died six years later, he was living at Hertford (probably with his son), and was buried there, contrary to the desire expressed in his will that he should be interred near his wife's relations at Hatfield.

By 1779 John Briant junior, then described as a whitesmith, had settled in the County Town, and in 1781 or '82, having gained the patronage of the Earl of Salisbury, he became tenant of one of the Earl's premises at Hertford (where Messrs. Simson Shand's printing works now is in Parliament Square). Here he set up his bellfoundry. One of Briant's early commissions was the repair of the clock in the turret of Hatfield House, and the casting of the dinner bell for the House. Amongst his first sets of bells was the peal of eight for his former parish church here at Hatfield, which were incidentally opened on 5th June, 1786—just two days before their maker's wedding-day.

Fig. 19. Briant's "No. 4" bell in Hatfield belfry, 1964.
(Photo: H. W. Gray).

Much has been written of Briant (see "John Briant," by H. C. Andrews, 1930). Suffice here to quote: his reputation "not only as a skilful founder, but as a most conscientious and honest man is widely known." "No man took such pains and trouble . . . . in turning out superior bells in perfect tune," and "often-times he would rather lose by a job than have the reflection that he had sent out a bad bell."

Having sold his Hatfield property about 1790, this Hertfordshire worthy died in straitened circumstances in 1829 at the age of eighty, after spending his last years in the Marlborough Almshouses, St. Albans. It is said that some years before his death, an admirer of his genius and industry expressed his regret to Briant that "he had not acquired a competency to run a carriage, when he (Briant) bluntly replied, 'I don't want a carriage. I'm satisfied with the station of life that God has placed me in. I've enjoyed more real pleasure in my favourite pursuits than the wealth of India could afford'."

A worthy epitaph to one of Hatfield's (if he may be so described) greatest craftsmen.

Papermakers

For well over eight hundred years, until about 1911, one of the fundamental trades of any community—the grinding of grain—was carried on at the Manor mills at Mill Green. This was not the only trade carried on at Mill Green however, for here also was Hatfield's papermaking industry.

It has been described in Book 6, p. 11, how the fulling mill built by Walter Morrell in 1608, for setting the poor to work, became a nuisance to Luke Rawson the miller, and how the scheme, though well intended, gradually dwindled. In 1638 the Earl of Salisbury leased all the mills at Mill Green (with other property) to Edward Arris, a London surgeon (see p. 79), who sub-leased the fulling mill to one Thomas Frewen, who appears in the Hearth Tax return of 1663 as living in the Ludwickhyde Ward of the parish (which included Mill Green). He was elsewhere described as a "brown-paper maker."

It appears to have been Frewen who turned the fulling-mill into a paper-mill. This was quite easy because the machinery for fulling consisted of great wooden hammers raised by the water-wheel which beat the dirt out of the cloth. They could equally well be used to pulp rags for paper, and at this time the pulping process was the only part of paper-making to be mechanised. The mill had certainly been converted to a paper-mill, employing both male and female labour, by 1663, for in May of that year we find that John Larence and Mary Turner, "two from the paper Mill from Hadfild" were married at Monken Hadley.

Hertfordshire had been a pioneer in paper-making, the first paper-mill in the country having been set up on the Lea at Hertford by John Tate in the 1490's. His mill produced paper of remarkably fine quality, but was probably forced to cease operations due to strong competition from abroad.

In 1696 a survey shows that there were then a hundred paper-mills in Great Britain, and by 1722 300,000 reams were being produced at £2. 10s. 0d. a ream.

Frewen was followed at Hatfield before 1691 by Isaac Moore, who in that year received from the Earl of Salisbury timber for the repair of the paper-mill. Other evidence points to the fact that Isaac had married Frewen's daughter Sarah, and following Moore's death the trade was carried on by *his* son-in-law John Archer. In 1730 Archer was paying £25 a year rent, but before his death in 1764 the rental had risen to £32 10s. 0d. Mrs. Archer continued the lease until her own death, when she left the implements and stock in trade of her business to her great-nephew, Isaac Moore. Perhaps Moore did not make a success of the concern, for soon after 1780 he was followed here by one Patrick Welch, a condition of whose tenure was that he should take the mill down and rebuild it. The Moore family did not move far away however, and in 1851 Isaac Moore's son, a gardener, was still living at Mill Green, and several of his descendants still live in the town today.

By 1788 the lease of the paper-mill had been obtained by Thomas Vallance, "an eminent wholesale stationer" of Cheapside, London, who like other stationers of that day, had found it desirable, and indeed necessary, to have the means of producing his own goods. For 43 years Vallance was one of the Common Council of the City of London, and as such must have known Cristopher Corrall the laceman, mentioned on page 55, although whether this connection influenced his coming to Hatfield is not known. In Vallance's time the rent of the mill rose to £50 per annum, probably occasioned by the recent rebuilding. He had not had the mill long, however, before it was burned down, and again rebuilt, and in 1790 came the strike threat of eleven of Vallance's employees (see page 55, and Book 6, page 17).

Following these misfortunes, in about 1796 Vallance took over the Pickford Mill, a few miles up the Lea, at Harpenden, letting the Hatfield mill to Thomas Creswick. Creswick bought the lease from Vallance in 1800, and proceeded to improve the mill considerably by installing a steam engine and other machinery worth about £15,000, which enabled him to produce paste boards, drawing boards and cards as well as paper.

All went well until a few years before Creswick's lease was due to expire in 1838. Because of some disagreement, the Marquess of Salisbury refused to renew the lease. Being compelled to find new premises, Creswick finally decided to transfer his business to Wandsworth, and began to remove his machinery. The Marquess instituted legal proceedings, on the grounds that all the machinery added to the mill became the property of the landlord, but the case was dismissed. Thus Hatfield's paper-making industry came to an end. Shortly before the mill's closure, the Rector, the Rev. F. J. Faithfull, had asked the Marquess to stop the paper-making because of the morals of the girls employed there —poor girls, they had only strolled through the lanes arm-in-arm, singing!

Although the effects of the paper-works had been removed, the mill was still described as "a paper-mill on the river" in 1849. For a short time the building was in use as an oil-mill, but as it never paid the project was abandoned, and the premises became two cottages which were later demolished to be replaced by the present house (picture, Book 6, p. 18). The row of red-brick cottages standing parallel to the Hertford Road are said to have been provided by Creswick for his workpeople.

The speciality of Creswick's mill was apparently hand-made writing paper, and it was to supervise its manufacture that Mark Powell, a paper-maker from Kent was employed in the 1830's. It must have been while living at the mill that he met Mary Bigg, sister of the miller at the neighbouring corn-mill. He married her in 1832 and a few years later left the paper-mill and set up in Fore Street, first as a stationer and later as a draper (p. 61 and Book 11a, p. 22).

As a footnote it might be added that the paper-mill with the corn-mills, and the many farms in the neighbourhood of Mill Green were, no doubt, the reason for Joseph Starkey setting up his smith's shop here, near the "Green Man," sometime before his death in 1838. (Earlier, in 1824, a James Starkey was occupier of a smithy at Wild Hill). Following Joseph's death, his widow and son Thomas carried on the family trade of smiths and machine makers. Over the years the family adapted their trade to a changing type of business, and today, although the mills are no longer active, and the many farms in the district have been almost all eaten away, the Starkey Engineering Company's workshops still carry on a wide range of general and precision engineering, on the site the family's smithy occupied over a century ago.

Wheelwrights and Smiths

Of Hatfield's wheelwrights the British Universal Directory of 1794 names but one—this was the business of the Palmer family in Park Street (see Book 11a, pp. 35-36). In 1823-4 however, Pigott's Directory shows two businesses here—Palmer's name had gone, but in its place we find Thomas Hadlin in the North Road, and Daniel Hagger in Pond Hill. By 1838 Hagger had apparently been succeeded in Pond Hill by Ebenezer Bunker, who carried on his wheelwright's craft where the new London Road was to be built in the early 1850's, just to the west of the "Dray Horse." After the building of the road Bunker took premises beside this new highway, at the corner of French Horn Lane. Here he expanded his wheelwright's trade and also went in for coach-building.

Fig. 20. Mr. James Gray.

It was following the death of Ebenezer Bunker, and of his son Henry in 1882 that the young James Gray took over the business. Although he had been born at Welwyn in 1860, and his parents later farmed at Queen Hoo Hall for many years, in coming to Hatfield James Gray was in fact but returning to his family home, for his father had been born here seventy years earlier. The Grays had been in the parish since 1783 when Daniel Gray, a labourer, married Martha Wray and settled down in the Wray's cottage at Dognell Green. This was the Daniel Gray whose ass was stolen in 1809 (Book 6, p. 21). In the early years of the 19th century

71

three of his nephews from Codicote followed him here—Richard Gray settling at Roe Green where he kept the "Old Fiddle," William living near his uncle at Dognell Green, and John farming in a small way at Hatfield Hyde. Descendants of all three brothers are still living in Hatfield, and it was William's grandson James who, having learnt the coachbuilder's and wheelwright's craft at Hertford, acquired the Bunkers' business in 1882.

Four years after taking over, "Jimmy" Gray pulled down the old shops and put up a new building, and four years later again he put up further works, these being followed by a new smith's and engineer's shop. In about 1907 the "St. James's Review" describing the business, stated that "now a fourth building has just been completed, which is far and away beyond anything yet attempted in the way of model structures in the town. The floor space provides garage for fifty cars, the upper storey, which has a 16ft. plate-glass window, being used for the manufacture of all descriptions of motor and carriage bodies.

"Nor does this altogether exhaust the capacity for work. Someway removed herefrom [in Park Street] is the department for heavy vans and carts and those demanded for farm and agricultural purposes. Then there is the cutting up and storage of wood, which is given effect to in the timber yard. The trees are felled and the trunks brought here, where they are sawn up and stored until the wood is thoroughly seasoned.

"All the ironwork employed in the constructional part of the work is made in the smiths' shop, which is fitted with the latest pattern screw-cutting lathes, drilling machines and various other appliances. Another department, where the wood is cut up and shaped for the bodies, wheels and shafts, is provided with further lathes, also band and circular saws. The various machinery throughout the building is driven by a powerful gas engine, which also works a dynamo for supplying electric light. This reminds us that there is a miniature half-horse power gas engine for charging electric accumulators, the point of interest being that the different parts were made and turned, and the engine completed in toto, by Mr. Gray's own workmen.

"Though motors are a very considerable part of the trade in force, they in no way overshadow the building of carriages and broughams: landaus, victorias, etc., are on exhibit in the showrooms, or can be built to order. A feature in this connection is a governess car, of circular shape and very deep, so as to secure both safety and comfort. It has also a sliding seat for the driver, which can be adapted for balancing the car.

"As regards motors, we may say that bodies of any shape, and upholstered in any style, can be fitted to any chassis, which, by the way, will be found more economical to purchasers than resort to West End depots. The quality of all work carried out is guaranteed to be of the best material and workmanship; and a visit of inspection is cordially invited by Mr. Gray, who will be pleased to give callers any further information. Repairs of all kinds are undertaken, and every requisite and accessory for motors supplied, especially oils, grease and tyres.

"This report is not by any means a detailed account of the various ramifications of the business, but sufficient has been said to show that Mr. Gray occupies a forefront position not merely in the commercial affairs of Hatfield, but in that of the coach-building trade and motor industry generally."

After "Jimmy" Gray's death in 1913 (he had been also, for twenty years, lieutenant, secretary and treasurer of the Hatfield Fire Brigade) his business was carried on by his two sons, but was sold in 1945 to the present proprietors, who still trade under the old name—indeed "a name as old as the motor industry."

Fig. 21. Part of Gray's Motor Works, London Road, about 1910.

Developing in the same way and at the same time as Gray's motor works was the business of the Waters family, which of course, like Gray's is still very much in evidence in the town. While Gray's had developed from a small wheelwright's trade, Waters's sprung from an old-established family smithy, and a link with this firm can be traced back to the early years of the 17th century. It is then that the name of Bamford first occurs in local records. Elizabeth daughter of Thomas Bamford was baptised here in 1614, and two years later her father was "presented" at the Archdeacon's Visitation "for carting wood on St. Michael's Day." In 1648 we hear of Thomas Bamford, an "iron-monger," when he obtained from the Earl of Salisbury the lease of the tolls of the markets and fairs to be held in Hatfield for the next sixty years (see Book 11a, p. 5). The term "ironmonger" may indicate that Thomas was indeed a blacksmith—if not, he must certainly have had an interest in the trade. From a deed of 1703 relating to "Priory House" Thomas Bamford (probably son of the "ironmonger") who is described as a "smith", appears as occupier of a house—and presumably also a smithy—which stood where the "Great Northern" Inn now is. This Thomas was followed at the same premises in about 1720 by Nathaniel Bamford, also a blacksmith. About a decade later Nathaniel moved to Duck Lane. His premises stood on the site of the present No. 4 Park Street, and here he was succeeded in the business by his son Thomas, who died in 1761 leaving a young family. Some seven years later his widow met and married John Baker, Farrier-Major in the Royal Horse Guards, who settled at Hatfield, living at the Bamford home in Duck Lane, and bringing up his three step-sons, Thomas, William and John as farriers and blacksmiths. These three brothers practised their craft in the town for a number of years—William leaving at the end of the century for Essendon, where his smith's business was carried on until about 1920 by three more generations of Bamfords.

In 1851 William's youngest son, Nathaniel is found as a veterinary surgeon at Woodside, while another son, William junior had returned to Hatfield and taken over the Barnes' family smithy, opposite the "Baker's Arms" at the top of Back Street. This smithy remained in Bamford's hands until about 1865, when Walter Waters took it over and traded there as blacksmith and wheelwright until the place was demolished in about 1895. Waters then moved his business to the old Militia Barracks in Batterdale, formerly the site of Hare's malting. Here Walter, with his two sons commenced building, selling and repairing cycles, motor-cycles and cars, laying the foundations of the present extensive business. In the early 1900's further premises were taken on the London Road at the southern end of the town, near Gray's works, and some years later a cycle shop was built opposite the "Dray Horse." About 1925 the Company acquired the old Pryor Reid Brewery premises, (Book 11a, fig. 16, p. 47), part of which they converted for use as their workshops and garage, while in the next decade further premises were built on the newly-constructed Barnet By-Pass.

Hatfield's two original firms of motor engineers can thus claim worthy ancestries, and although neither developed into a Ford or Morris enterprise, they did keep the town abreast of the times in the early part of the century, and were the forerunners of the numerous other light-engineering firms that have since come to the district.

Local Boy Makes Good

A success story which must have been well-known to 18th century Hatfield, but has since been entirely forgotten, is that of John Church. Christened here in February, 1724-5, he was the second surviving son of Thomas Church, described as a "labourer" and tenant of a cottage and a few acres at Woodside. Here young John grew up with his brothers and sisters (one of whom, Alice, married Daniel Deacon, a local weaver, who in 1773 was presented at the Quarter Sessions for having assaulted his wife).

Nothing seems to be known of John's early life, or how he came to make his way to London. He had certainly made a place for himself in the City by 1756, when he was appointed a trustee of his cousin Daniel Haydon's marriage settlement. By then he must already have obtained a position as clerk in the famous banking house of Messrs. Child &

Co., of Temple Bar, and about 1763 he was admitted a partner in the bank — no mean achievement. Within a few years he was in a position to return to Hatfield and buy— not the cottage he had lived in as a boy— but the nearby landed estate of Woodside Place itself. He enlarged the estate and re-built the old Tudor house. The large coaching inn which went with the estate he re-named the "Greyhound"— from the charges in his newly assumed coat of arms.

Another nice touch is added when John, having made his place in the world, had occasion to look up the entry of his christening in the parish registers. Finding his mother's name wrongly entered, he caused the following correction to be made: "The Christian Name of Mrs. Church, the Mother of John, baptis'd Feby. 28, was Mary and is therefore alter'd by Tho: Marsham, Curate, at the desire of me Jno Church" (signed).

Fig. 22. Woodside Place, 1839. From a drawing by J. Buckler in the County Record Office, Hertford.

(*Photo: H. W. Gray*).

At Woodside Place and at his Temple Bar residence (he also owned an estate at Battersea) he spent his remaining years. Dying a bachelor in 1788, he "left his fortune which was very considerable, to his numerous relations," while his Woodside house "and estate of £1,000 a year" (Gentleman's Magazine) went to his brother William and his wife.

On John's death the Church connection with Child's Bank ceased, and the following generations lived the lives of country gentlemen and farmers, at Woodside (see also Book 9, p. 26).

In the 19th century this same family produced an eminent doctor, William Selby Church (old John's great-great-nephew), who was three times President of the Royal College of Physicians (1899-1905), and was created a Baronet in 1901. Sir William also took a keen interest in more local affairs, was amongst other things a County Councillor and Chairman of Hatfield R.D.C. (1901-1919). His elder son was one of the 141 local men who lost their lives in the first World War, and the family is now represented by the younger son, Sir Geoffrey Church, formerly Chairman of the Hatfield Magistrates, who still lives at Woodside, at the former "Greyhound" Inn, not half a mile from the site of the original cottage of old Thomas Church.

The Post Office

The earliest evidence we have of the postal services at Hatfield is the cover of a letter written on January 8th, 1756, by Mr. Hutchinson, of Woodhall, to his solicitor in London. This has the post mark 'HATFIELD' on it, and another stamp $^9/_{1A}$ which may either be that of the despatching or of the receiving office. At this date the Royal Mail was carried by post-boys on relays of horses, and as there was a posting station for fresh horses at the "White Lyon" (afterwards the "Salisbury Arms") at Hatfield, it would be a suitable place for a post office, though we do not know when this first opened. Certainly the 1761 militia return shows two post-boys, Thomas Robinson and Isaac Deer, apparently at the "White Lyon", while William Lewis, also a post-boy was at the "Chequers" at the bottom of Fore Street. From 1780 to 1785 John Farraway (at the "Chequers" in 1773) and William Darlington were employed as post-boys.

At that time the cost of a letter to London was fivepence, and the same to St. Albans, although there was no direct postal route and letters had to go in to London and out again. In the summer of 1785 Mail Coaches first passed through Hatfield, travelling on the route between London and Nottingham, and the mail was carried by coach until the coming of the railway in 1850. An old railway photograph (in the possession of Mr. H. Musson) shows mail being collected and delivered by a mechanical arrangement of nets and hooks while the train was at speed, and Jim Thomas, then Head Postman, waiting at the side of the line to take up the incoming mail bag.

The first Post Master we know of was Ganzelius Miller, landlord of the "Salisbury Arms" (then the "White Lyon"), who about 1757 had unsuspectingly cashed a stolen private-bank note, a story which is told in the "Annual Register" for 1758. The Post Office appears to have remained at the same inn, and William Holden's bill-head, in use in 1784 carried the words 'The Post Office' (Book 3, fig. 5). Holden was followed by his son-in-law John Mawe who, when he left the Inn about 1795, appears to have taken the Post Office with him, probably to the second of the cottages which formerly stood in front of the present Rectory in Fore Street—it was certainly here in the 1820's to 1840's when it was run by Mawe's daughters, Miss Mary and Miss Ruth, and by their brother Harry.

In the 1820's letters could be sent daily to London, Leeds and Glasgow, and the London Mail called at Hatfield at 10-30 p.m. on its way north, the southbound coach having passed through two-and-a-half hours earlier. The scene outside the Post Office of that day is described by Charles Dickens in "Oliver Twist"—Bill Sykes "turned back up the town and getting out of the glare of the lamps of a stage coach that was standing in the street, was walking past, when he recognised the Mail from London, and saw that it was standing at the little post-office . . . . The guard was standing at the door, waiting for the letter bag, 'Now look alive there, will you' said the guard, 'Damn that 'ere bag, it warn't ready night afore last. This won't do, you know!'" This incident was supposed to take place in 1835.

By 1839 a "cross-post" had been established to St. Albans and Hertford. Letters arrived from London at 10-0 p.m., but there were two posts a day into London, at 4-0 p.m. and 3-0 a.m.! The post-box, however, was closed at nine at night.

The building of the railway, and the increase in business probably encouraged the transfer of the Post Office to the shop of Mark Powell, the draper (Book 11a, p. 22), near the bottom of the Street, for it was here, with Powell as Post Master by the time of the 1851 census. It was allotted the official number 343, which was used on the post marks of the time. The number signified that this was an Official Post Office receiving an average of 100 letters a week, and daily deliveries of mail were permitted. Hatfield's delivery was at 8-0 a.m. The post box now closed a little later, at 9-30 p.m., but even after that letters could be received up to ten o'clock on payment of an extra penny. Ten years later there were two morning deliveries of mail, and by 1874 three a day, at 7-0 a.m., 9-20 a.m. and 6-15 p.m. Mark Powell's office served for the post, money orders, as a telegraph office, for Government Annuities and insurance.

In 1875 Powell was succeeded as Postmaster by James Benjamin Dunham, a man of many parts in 19th century Hatfield, whose family still lives in the town. Four deliveries a day were being made three years after Dunham took over, and in 1885 he moved to a new Post Office adjoining the "Salisbury" Hotel in London Road, which had just been built. In 1886 he advertised "Continental mail received daily up to 4-15", and by 1890 there was a Post Office Savings Bank.

By 1885 we hear of three "wall letter boxes", at Newton (sic), cleared twice a day, and Woodfield and Woodside cleared every afternoon. Two others, at the Railway station and at Hatfield Park were there by 1886, and are still in use.

Due to the "phenomenal growth of Hatfield", in the 1930's a new Post Office "became imperative", and in May, 1936, the Crown Post Office opposite the Station was opened—although four years before this the Rural Council were asking for the building to be speeded up because of unemployment.

In New Town a Post Office was established by 1899, with Jonathan Tingey as sub-postmaster (see also Book 11a, pp. 44-45). This later moved to the greengrocers' then kept in the first Right of Way by Mrs. Savill and her husband, a postman. In the early 1930's they moved their business, together with the Post Office to 81 St. Albans Road, where it remained until the Crown Post Office was built in White Lion Square in 1961. This then became the Head Post Office instead of the 1936 Office in the Great North Road, where the sorting accommodation was no longer adequate.

Hatfield Professionals

What a very odd thing, sir; here, all in a row,
Live, the doctor, the lawyer, the parson!
Such professional men, in a word I will shew,
Contribute much good to the nation.
A plethoric compress, or a whirligig head,
Our doctor will promptly set right sir;
Cathartics are ready, if his lancet we dread,
Or he quickly prepares us a blister.
For a settlement, deed, or licence to wed,
At the very next door we may enter;
To convey an estate, or get one instead,
We go to the house in the centre.
Now next to the lawyer's we find out the priest,
Who, mentioned the last, is by no means the least;
If his morals be good, and he preach from the heart,
His employ is as useful—set joking apart.

These amusing verses, which appeared in the "Herts Mercury" in 1826, show that while the butcher, baker and candlestick maker still practised their trades in Fore Street, the professional class was by then well established in the larger houses at the top of the Street. The parson referred to was the Rev. Benjamin Peile, the curate, who then lived at the Vicarage (the present Rectory), where he ran a small private school; the doctor was Thomas Osbaldeston, at the present "Greenaway," while in between lived—until he moved to St. Albans following his marriage in 1830—Francis James Osbaldeston, the local attorney and County Coroner (Book 11a, fig. 2).

There were lawyers practising in the Town before this—John Palmer was here throughout the second half of the 18th century, while Thomas Arthur, gentleman, who died in 1740, and whose name appears in several deeds and settlements and as witness to numerous wills over a period of fifty years, was probably the local attorney. Prior to this, however, Hatfield does not seem to have possessed a resident lawyer, and from about 1640 till his death in 1697, Richard Wilkinson, schoolmaster and parish clerk, was in constant demand in the district to assist in making wills and drawing up deeds. Before Wilkinson's time, these duties were usually performed by his predecessors as parish clerk, or by the parson.

As far as the medical profession is concerned, during the past three centuries the people of Hatfield seem to have been well provided for—that is, for those who could afford their services. Just as the legal profession had originally sprung from the ranks of the clergy, so too did the practitioners of medicine. In the Middle Ages most physicians had been clerics, but the Church's disapproval of the shedding of blood by the clergy, left surgery to laymen, who by the 14th century had formed a guild in London. In 1540 the Guild of Barbers, who too had long practised the healing of wounds and drawing of teeth, amalgamated with the Guild of Surgeons to form the Company of Barber-Surgeons, a marriage that lasted two hundred years. From the early 16th century the practice of medicine was strictly controlled, those not having a University degree having to be licensed, as regards physicians, by the Royal College of Physicians, or in the case of surgeons (as also were midwives and schoolmasters) by the Diocesan Bishop.

In a Quarter Sessions Roll of 1594 we hear of Edward Duffyll, chirurgion of Hatfield. Nearly half a century later occurs the first of a series of distinguished medical men connected with Hatfield. This was Edward Arris, Serjeant-Surgeon to the King (an office still in existence), alderman of London, and sometime Master of the Barber-Surgeons' Company, who in the mid-seventeenth century leased property here from the Earl of Salisbury (see p. 69). A surgeon and benefactor of St. Bartholomew's Hospital, he was founder of the Arris Lecture, which is still given at the Royal College of Surgeons. Although it is doubtful whether he ever practised at Hatfield, his elder son, Dr. Thomas Arris certainly did at St. Albans, for which Borough he was for eighteen years M.P.

Throughout much of the 17th century, however, the Town was served by two (possibly three) generations of the Longstaff family, as resident barber-surgeons. Although the surgeons of those days did not enjoy the status they do today, and together with the apothecaries, were generally very much the poor relations of the physicians, during the next century, as their skill developed, their lot improved. In 1667 we hear that William Longstaff (himself not a surgeon), his wife and three small children, were found to be reduced to great want, and must either perish or be a charge on the parish, without the payment of £100 which was due to them. William's brother, John Longstaff, the barber-surgeon, however was somewhat better off. At his death in 1711 he owned a house in the "High Street"—though he actually lived in one of Lord Salisbury's houses which formerly stood in front of the present Rectory —and was able to leave legacies totalling £500 to his various relations (two of whom were in business respectively as a butcher and a tailor). A later member of the family, Ann Longstaff, was described when she died in 1776, as "Sexton of this Parish."

The inventory of John Longstaff's goods made after his death, reveals that his seven-roomed house was not lavishly furnished: his total effects were valued at only £13 6s. 0d. However his Executors held £50, together with bonds for sums owing him—£50 from Nicholas Ludford and £450 from Dr. Thomas Fuller, the Rector (one wonders what occasioned the loan of this amount to the Rector). Longstaff's "shopp" (his surgery) offered little comfort—in it was found only a little looking Glass, a little kettle of Tin, one brass warmeing pann, 2 brass basons, a pair of Andirons, and an old chair, together valued at six shillings. His barber's apron was found in the "first Chamber", and "a little Cabbinet with Surgeon's Instruments" was kept in the "Second Chamber."

Apparently of somewhat higher standing was the practice, still in existence today, which is clearly traceable back to one John Heaviside in the mid-1700's, and may even be descended from the Longstaffs' practice. Heaviside was a member of an interesting north country family which had come south in the 17th century, and prospered. One of his cousins was "an eminent saddler in Bishopsgate Street", another was in partnership with the Master Carpenter to H.M's. Ordnance (leaving at his death in 1775 legacies of £14,620), while a third member of the family was Master of the Ceremonies at Bath in the early 19th century.

John Heaviside himself, was in 1743 living at Barnet, but by the time of his marriage to Mary Elliott two years later had settled at Hatfield. Although he is the earliest definite member of the practice, it is perhaps significant that in May, 1744, Bartholomew Spurling, a local surgeon who lived in Fore Street (now no. 9), had died. On coming to Hatfield, Heaviside took the lease of the former "George" Inn, at the top of Back Street, and here he lived till his retirement three decades later (when he appears to have lived at Goldings Farm). A fine memorial to him by Thomas Banks, erected in the parish church by his son, John Heaviside, Surgeon Extraordinary to George III, records his virtues, and that he, "to the manifold advantage of this place, and the general benefit of no narrow circuit, was for more than thirty years a resident surgeon in this Town."

As appears from local wills of the period, Heaviside seems to have been the trusted friend of many local folk. At the time of making his own will, he had in his hands over £10,000 trust monies belonging to various people. He died in 1787, and in his will desired "to be decently but privately buried as thinking it improper and indecent to make any parade with a dead cor[p]se." His humanity is further shown by his wish that the debts owing him should be "collected in by my Executor with as much tenderness to those who owe them as is possible."

On Heaviside's retirement—probably in 1773—the practice was acquired (apparently as part of his marriage settlement) for James Penrose, a young surgeon, and descendant of an old Cornish family. Penrose also took over from Heaviside the lease of the "George," together with a considerable amount of farm land. The value of the practice at this time can be judged from the fact that "as a satisfaction to the said John Heaviside for his quitting the Business and profits of his profession," James Penrose, together with his father (Francis Penrose, also a surgeon and noted medical writer) and his father-in-law (James Bellis, a jeweller and toyman of Pall Mall, and of Hatfield Woodside) stood bound to Heaviside and his heirs in the sum of £500 and interest. By 1788—the year after Heaviside's death—the bond had not been fully discharged, although the debt was cleared in the next few years.

In 1789 Penrose removed from the old inn (which was soon afterwards pulled down), and obtained from Lord Salisbury the lease of the house now known as "Northcotts." Here he remained till his death, and here his widow spent her remaining years.

In 1793 Penrose was honoured by being appointed Surgeon Extraordinary to George III and Surgeon to His Majesty's Household, an office he held for 25 years. (It was perhaps not entirely a coincidence that the Lord Salisbury of this time was Lord Chamberlain).

Penrose was joined in the Hatfield practice in about 1800 by his second wife's nephew, Carr Ellison Lucas, then in his twenties. In 1801 the young surgeon married his master's daughter Henrietta, who died eight years later. On Dr. Penrose's death in 1818, he was buried, according to his own wishes, near his daughter in Hatfield churchyard (where his tomb can still be seen). The practice was carried on by his son-in-law, Lucas, who the following year was granted the degree of M.D. by the Archbishop of Canterbury.

In 1805 Dr. Lucas had his residence at another old inn—this time at the former "King's Head" at the foot of Fore Street, but in the 1820's the practice operated from the North Road (probably at "Northcotts"). Dr. Lucas had an only son who after being educated at St. Paul's School and Eton, Oxford and Cambridge, studied medicine in London, in preparation presumably, for joining his father's practice. Lucas, however, having lost his young wife after only eight years of marriage, had the misfortune in 1830 to lose also this, his only son (aged 26). He gave up his practice and retired to Devon, where he died at the age of 80, in 1858.

In about 1815 William Lloyd Thomas, a young surgeon from Gloucester, had come to Hatfield. By the early 1820's he had become Dr. Lucas's partner, and following the latter's retirement, he carried on the practice. About the time of his marriage in 1830, Lloyd Thomas moved to the present "North Place" (which before this had for many years been the Curate's residence) and here the practice remained well into the present century. Being medical attendant to the Cecil family, in 1835 he had the melancholy task of identifying the remains of the Dowager Marchioness of Salisbury, who perished in the fire which destroyed part of Hatfield House. In 1843 Lloyd Thomas was elected a founder-Fellow of the Royal College of Surgeons.

The year 1848 must have been one of some apprehension for the people of Hatfield; Arthur Hankin noted in his diary that there was "great talk of the end of the world, to take place on March 31st." Having survived this, the town was struck the same year by a severe smallpox epidemic, and it was apparently to help deal with this that Dr. Thomas was joined by Charles Drage, a young surgeon from St. Bartholomew's Hospital. The crisis over, Drage remained at Hatfield, soon becoming Lloyd Thomas's partner in the practice, and in 1854 history repeated itself when he married Thomas's only daughter, Elinor Margaret. On the death of his father-in-law the next year, Charles Drage became sole owner of the practice.

Dr. Drage soon developed a large London practice in addition to that at Hatfield, and as a young man is said to have attended the great Duke of Wellington—the first of four Prime Ministers to be his patients (the others being the Lords Melbourne and Palmerston of Brocket Hall, and Lord Salisbury). He is remembered by many of his patients still living in Hatfield, being famous alike for the blind faith he inspired in his patients and for the forthrightness of his utterances at meetings of the British Medical Association. He "cured" diphtheria with "massive doses of port wine," dismissed clinical thermometers as "nasty, scarey things," and particularly abominated fashionable gynaecologists.

At eighty, Dr. Drage was at the height of his powers and seven years later was considering the possibility of total retirement,

Fig. 23. Dr. Charles Drage.
(*Photo in possession of R. L. Drage*).

having previously been prevented from taking such a step by the demands of equally elderly patients who flatly refused to accept any younger man in his place. After ten years of well-earned retirement, he died in 1922—three years short of his century.

Following family tradition, Dr. Drage's eldest son, after a period as house-surgeon at St. Bartholomew's, had joined his father in practice at Hatfield in 1885. Equally as forthright and blunt as the elder Dr. Drage, he practised here for 33 years, predeceasing his father in 1919.

Following Lovell Drage's death, the practice was carried on for a number of years at North Place by Dr. Ballance, and is now in the hands of Dr. Kenneth Hutchin and Partners.

Another line of local doctors can be traced from Samuel Atkinson, an apothecary (a prescriber and seller of drugs), who in 1714 married Grace Searancke, the brewer's daughter (Book 11a, fig. 2). The year after his marriage Atkinson purchased a house in Fore Street (now No. 16)—which incidentally had not many years before belonged to James Lowen, a surgeon—and here he lived till his death in 1767. Of his sons, Samuel moved to Hertford, and was later appointed County Coroner, while John, the second son, practised as a surgeon in Hatfield until his father's death, when he moved to Hitchin. Following the elder Atkinson's death, the family residence was let to John Darby, both a surgeon and apothecary, who presumably had acquired the Atkinsons' practice.

In 1777 Darby, perhaps wanting to live in his own house, or maybe to gain the franchise by becoming a freeholder, bought two houses on the opposite side of the street, which he proceeded to re-build as one house, fit for the prosperous surgeon he was. This is the house, known today as "Greenaway." In his will Darby left legacies amounting to several thousand pounds, and included £100 for the use of the "Medical Society."

Meanwhile, next door (at the present Morton House) lived another surgeon, Thomas Osbaldeston (his wife was a granddaughter of the apothecary Samuel Atkinson—Book 11a, fig. 2), who, it seems likely, had been Darby's partner. When Osbaldeston died in 1837, his elder son Thomas junior, carried on the surgery and made his home after his father's death at Mr. Darby's former house. The younger Thomas's son (Dr. Lyttleton Osbaldeston) transferred the surgery to "Triangle House," Batterdale, and died in 1897. The practice was then acquired by Dr. Percy Morgan Brittain, a physician well-known and well-loved in Hatfield for the next 38 years till his death in 1935—"the poorer his patients were, the kinder he was to them." The practice (now Dr. O'Neill's) has been carried on to the present time in the same premises.

By a coincidence, the old residence of Darby and the Osbaldestons was later the home of yet another doctor in the late 19th century (Dr. Hall), and is now the home of a fourth—Dr. Kenneth Hutchin, senior partner in the practice founded by John Heaviside.

Continuity Continues

Dr. Hall, who after leaving the old doctor's house in Fore Street carried on his practice at Priory House (fig. 18), was a member of an old Hatfield family, originally carpenters and builders in the town. William Hall, born here in 1741, carried on the trade of a carpenter and builder in the town (he lived at the "Old School House," now "Church Cottage") till his death in 1794. He left three children, a daughter who married the butcher George Walby (Book 11a, fig. 9), James Hall who died a few years after his father, and William Hall, the elder son, who carried on the builder's business, and who in the first half of the 19th century succeeded the Searanckes as principal landlord (apart from Lord Salisbury) of the town properties. It was probably the younger William who built for himself "Hill House", the fine late Georgian residence in Park Street, now somewhat over-shadowed by the Victorian viaduct (fig. 24).

On William's death in 1845, the Hall building business ceased, his only son having qualified as a surgeon and settled at Tottenham. But family ties once again proved too strong to be broken altogether, and two of the surgeon's children later returned to the town of their fore-bears—Mrs. Caesar, a widow, whose two daughters resided at "Galley-croft" until recent years, and Dr. Charles Hall. After more than thirty

Fig. 24. Hill House, from the Viaduct—the home of the Hall family.
(Photo: H. W. Gray, 1960).

years' practice in Hatfield, Dr. Hall retired to London, never to return, until his body was brought back to Hatfield for burial in the family vault in 1923.

At this time the character of Hatfield had changed little since the 1850's, the coming of the railway and building of the first New Town. The families of a century or more's standing still predominated. The old-established brewery had recently closed, but tradesmen and shopkeepers still sold their wares in Fore Street and Park Street; Dr. Hall's cousins, the Walby's, still had their butcher's shop in Park Street, the street in which they had practised their craft for two centuries or more. Great changes, however, were soon to take place.

By one of the odd coincidences of family history, it was another of Dr. Hall's cousins, whose name was soon to become as familiar as any in the whole of Hatfield's history, who at this date was engaged, not many miles away, in a new, specifically 20th-century craft, soon to become a great industry, the consequences of which were eventually to change the face of Hatfield beyond recognition. This pioneer's name? Geoffrey de Havilland.

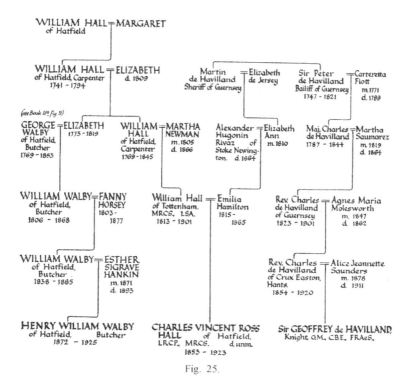

Fig. 25.

85

ANALYSIS OF TRADES FOR THE OLD PARISH OF HATFIELD

	1761 Militia Return	1794 Directory		1854 Directory			1899 Directory		
		(singly)	(with 1 other trade)	(singly)	(with 1 other trade)	(with 2 other trades)	(singly)	(with 1 other trade)	(with 2 other trades)
1. NOBILITY, GENTRY & CLERGY.	1	6		19	1		60	13	
2. FARMERS & AGRICULTURAL TRADES.									
Farmers	15	16	3	10	7	1	18	4	1
Bailiffs			1				3		
Cattle dealers and Salesmen				1			2	1	
Corn Merchants, Mealmen, Hay and Straw dealers	1		1		2		1	1	1
Cowkeepers & Dairymen & Milkmen		1					1	1	
Forester							1		
Gamekeepers	2			1			1		
Gardeners	2						2		
Horse Keeper	1								
Millers	6	2			2			2	
Pig Killer		1							
Shepherds	1								
Tasker	1								
Water Cress Grower							1		
	29	20	4	12	12	1	30	9	2
3. CRAFTSMEN.									
BUILDERS :							2		1
Brickmakers	1						1		
Bricklayers	5		1	2					
Carpenters and Joiners	11	5		2					2
Plumbers and Glaziers & Paperhanger	3	2		2			2	1	
MISCELLANEOUS :									
Basket Maker		1							
Boot & Shoemakers (Cordwainers in 1794)	5	3		6			5	1	
Clockmaker				1			1		
Coachbuilder, wheelwright & tyresmith							1		
Collarmakers	1	1							
Coopers			1		1				
Fellmonger	1								
Oil miller				1					
Paper maker	1								
Saddlers, harness & Collar makers	1		2	2			2		
Scale makers	1								

	1761 Militia Return	1794 Directory		1854 Directory			1899 Directory		
		(singly)	(with 1 other trade)	(singly)	(with 1 other trade)	(with 2 other trades)	(singly)	(with 1 other trade)	(with 2 other trades)
3. CRAFTSMEN (cont.)									
Shoeing smiths, farriers, etc.	8	3		2			5		1
Shoeing smith & machine maker				1					
Smith and cycle maker							1		
Stay and Corset maker				1					
Tanners	2	1							
Wheelwrights	2	1		1					1
	42	17	4	21	1		20	2	5
4. DISTRIBUTION TRADES, FOOD, CLOTHING, ETC.									
CLOTHING:									
Drapers and Tailors and Clothiers	7	6		5	2	1	3		
Dress makers (mantua maker)		1		2			3		
Milliners (Straw hat and bonnet maker)				1			1		
Breeches maker	1	1							
Weaver	1	1							
Shoe warehouse		1							
FOOD:									
Bakers	3	2		4	1		8	1	
Butchers	5	5		2	4		5	1	
Brewers and Maltsters	4	2			5		1		
Fishmongers		1		2			2		
Grocers and Tea dealers		1	1	2		1	3	1	1
Wine & Spirit Merchant							1		1
Inns, Hotels, Public houses	16	8	4	19	12		31	4	
Ostlers, Postboys, Waiters	11								
Tripeman		1							
Confectioner				1					
Refreshment Rooms							2	1	
Apartments, Lodging houses, etc.				1			3		
Chemist & druggists						2			1
China, glass & earthenware dealers				1			2		1
Ironmongers									1
Furniture and antique furniture dealers									2
Coal, coke and firewood dealers			1				1	1	1
Stationer & newsagent						1			1
Tallow Chandlers	2		1						
Shopkeepers (unclassified)		10	2	8	6		9	2	
	50	40	9	48	30	5	75	11	9

	1761 Militia Return	1794 Directory		1854 Directory			1899 Directory		
		(singly)	(with 1 other trade)	(singly)	(with 1 other trade)	(with 2 other trades)	(singly)	(with 1 other trade)	(with 2 other trades)
5. MISCELLANEOUS, SERVICES, ETC.									
Agents for Fire and Life Insurance Coys.						2	2		1
Agent to G.N.R.				1					
Auctioneer & Valuer				1					
Barbers (peruke maker)	3	2		2			2		
Carriers	3			1					
Chimney sweep				1					
Coachman	1								
Doctors, Surgeons, Apothercaries	2	2		4			4		
Higgler	1								
Hirer of Horses				1					
Omnibus proprietor				1					
Public officials			2	5	2	1	5	2	3
Schoolmasters & mistresses (private only in 1899).	1	2		6	1		1		
Surveyors & Architects		1	1				1		
Usher	1								
Veterinary Surgeon							1		
Florist							1		
Undertakers									3
Contractor							1		
Cycle agent							1		
Organist & proff. of music							1		
Banker							1		
Building Society							1		
Drill Instructor								1	
Stewards, Agents & Private Secretaries	1			1			3		
Station Master				1			1		
District Superintendent G.N.R.							1		
Lodgekeepers							2		
	13	7	3	24	4	3	29	3	7
TOTAL	135	90	20	124	48	9	214	38	23

Total Population of Hatfield   2,442 (1801)   3,862 (1851)   4,752 (1901)

N.B.: The Militia Return (of 1761) purports to be a list of all able bodied men between ages of 18 and 50 in the parish, eligible for Militia Service, and therefore is not intended to include all tradesmen then in the parish (there were 229 labourers and servants as well as the trades noted in this analysis).

The Militia Return shows numbers of journeymen as well as master-craftsmen, whereas the Directories only list the masters.

HENRY W. GRAY.

INDEX

This is the combined index for Part 11A (pages 1-48) and Part 11B (pages 49-99).

Note: Page numbers in *italics* indicate illustrations; page references in **boldface** indicate major treatment of a topic.

Batterdale House
(Colonel's House) 3,
37-8, *37*, 66
Bayden, Ann 16
Bean, Henry 63
Beard, William *12*, 15,
19, 29
Beasney, Elizabeth 16
Beasney, James *12*, 16,
29, 39
Beasney, John 16, 28, 29
Beasney, Thomas *12*, 16,
28
Beasney (Bestney) family
28-9
Bedwell Manor 9, 59
Bell Bar 8, 59
Bellis, James 81
bells 66-8, *68*
Bene, Richard 63
Bernard the potter 63
Berry, Mary 56
Bibby, James 29
Bibles 62
Bigg, Anthony 60
Bigg, Edward 60
Bigg, Freeman 60
Bigg, John 60
Bigg, Joseph 11, 61, *65*
Bigg (later Powell), Mary
22, 61, 70
Bigg, Richard 60
Bigg, William 60
Biggs family 60-2
Birchwood Farm 61, 62
Bishop's Hatfield 38
blacksmiths *12*, 73-4
Bligh, George 43
Bligh, John 43
Bligh family 43
Board of Guardians 46
boarding school 25
Bosford, William 64
Bowne, Hy. *12*
Bracey (railway
employee) 40
Bradshaw, George 13
breach of promise 15
bread
as legacy 13
breeches-maker *12*, 40, 87
breweries 9, 11, 13, 36,
43, 59, 62, 74, 85

brewers 10, 87
Brewhouse Farm 9
Briant, John 67-8
brickfields 63
Brickhill Close 63
bricklayers *12*, 34, 43, 44,
63-4, 65, 86
brickmakers 16, 36, 63-6,
86
Brickwall Hill 61
*British Universal
Directory* 71
Brittain, Dr. Percy
Morgan 83
Brocket, Sir John 55
Brocket Hall 54
Brocket Park 58, 61
Broomfields 66
Brown, Henry 29
Brown, Mary 56
Bryan, Isaac 63
Buckhamwykhyde *see*
Woodside
Buckler, John
drawing *75*
builders *12*, 34, 35, 36,
39, 41, 63-6, 84, 86
family pedigrees 42
table 34
Building Society 88
Bull Inn 59
Bunker, Ebenezer 71
Bunker, Henry 71
Burgess, James 39, 66
Burgess, William 66
Bury, Oliver 40
butchers *12*, 14, 16, 24,
25, 28-9, **31-3**, 40,
43, 84, 85, 87
Walby pedigree 30
Butler, Messrs. 14
By-Pass 66, 74

C

Caesar (*née* Hall), Mrs. 84
"California" *see* New
Town
Calverly (Caveller),
Henry 64
candlestick maker 3
Canham, Joseph 66
Canham, Sophia 26, 30
Carnbrook, Agnes 55, 56

Carpenter, Agnes 13
Carpenter, Edmond 13
carpenters 26, 35, 43, 84,
86
carriers 25, 88
cars 72, 74
Carter, Francis *12*
caterer 26, 42
cattle dealers 86
cattle prices 29
Causton, Mr. (printer) 15
Caveller, Hugh 16
Caveller family 7, 16
Cecil, Lady Gwendolen
38
Cecil family 7, 82
see also Salisbury
Cecil Mill 61
censuses 54
1851 55, 65, 77
centenarian 35
Chalkley, Mary 30
Chamber of Trade 46
chandlers 15, 29, 87
Chantry Farm 8, 27
Chapman, Charles James
34
Chapman, Dorcas 30
Chapman, Eliza Marian
34
Chapman, James (*d.
1816*) 65
Chapman, James (*b.1763*)
12, 34
Chapman, James (*b.1782*)
34
Chapman, John (*b. 1796*)
27, 34
Chapman, John (*b. 1818*)
34, 43
Chapman, Lucy 34
Chapman, Sarah
Elizabeth 34
Chapman, Sophia 34
Chapman, Thomas 34
Chapman, William 34
Chapman family 36, 65-6,
65
Chapman's Field 66
Chapman's Terrace 36
Cheek, Nathaniel 13
chemists 23-4, 87

Guild of Barbers 79
Grovestock, Richard 42
Grovestock family 42, 43
Grubb, Ann 15, 16
Grubb, Joshua 16

H

Hadlin, Thomas 71
Hagger, Daniel 71
hairdressers 27
Hakes, Elizabeth 56
Hall, Dr. (late *19c.*) 83, 84
Hall, Dr. Charles 13, 84-5
Hall, Charles Vincent
  Ross 85
Hall, Elizabeth 30
Hall, James 84
Hall, Margaret 85
Hall, William *12*, 32, 84,
  85
Hall family 9, 84, 85
Hamilton, Emilia 84
Handside 60
  Lower Handside Farm
  60
  Upper Handside Farm
  59
Hankin, Ann Maria 26
Hankin, Arthur 82
Hankin, Arthur William
  26, 27, 43
Hankin, Charles 26, 43
Hankin, Esther Sigrave
  30, 85
Hankin, Ethel 26
Hankin, Frederick John
  26, 27
Hankin, Henry 26, 27
  shop 27, *28*
Hankin, Henry Hudson
  26, 27, 28
Hankin, John (of
  Baldock) 26
  shop 27, *28*
Hankin, John (draper,
  d.1897) 26, 27
Hankin, Joseph 26
Hankin, Mary Ann Sarah
  10
Hankin, Oliver 26
Hankin, Rosa 26
Hankin, Sarah 26
Hankin, Sophia 26

Hankin, Stanley Coles 26,
  27
Hankin, William (glover
  and tailor, *d.1851*)
  26, 27, 28
Hankin, William (tailor,
  d.1870) 26
Hankin family pedigree
  26
Hardum, Charles 15
Hardum, Joseph 28
Hardum, Lancelot *12*, 14-
  15, 19
Hardum, Thomas 14, 15
Hare, Edward 10, 33
Hare, Rev. Samuel 10
Hare, Samuel 10, 33, 36-
  7, 66
Hare, Susannah 33
Hare family 9, 36, 52
  property owned by *8*
Harker (railway
  employee) 40
Harpenden 58, 70
Harrow, Andrew 64
Harrow, John 64
Harrow, William 64
Harrow, William (Fudge)
  64
Harrow family 63-4
Harper family 25
Harrow, John 38
Hart, John 25
Hart, William *12*, 24, 32
Hart family 24-5
Harvey, Thomas 15
hat makers 87
Hatfield, Manor of 4
Hatfield Brewery 9, 11,
  36, *47*
Hatfield House
  archives 5
  bell and clock 67
  building 63
  fire 82
Hatfield Hyde 61, 72
Hatfield Mill 61
Hatfield Park 78
Hawkins, William 25
Haydon, Daniel 75
Hayfield Thorpe 59
Hearth Tax 69
Heaviside, John 80-1, 83

Henry VIII, King 59
Hertford 9, 67, 69
  Assizes 64
Hertfordshire County
  Council 60
Hertingfordbury 57, 59
Hertford 9
Hertford Mercury 41
Herts Mercury 78
Hertfordshire Militia 38,
  43
Hickson, Emily 34
Hickson, Sarah Sophia 34
Hickson, Thomas 34
higgler 88
High Street *see* Fore
  Street
highwaymen 64
Hill, Elizabeth 56
Hill, Helen 56
Hill, Nicholas 55, 56, 57
Hill, Thomas 56
Hill, William, Senior 55,
  56
Hill, William (*d.1593*) 56
Hill family 27
Hill House 36, 40, 84, *84*
Hinton, John 67
Holden, William 77
Hollingsworth, Mary 56
Hollingsworth, William
  17
Holly Bush messuage 31
Holwell Manor 40
Holwellhyde 59
Home Farm 31, 36
hops 18
Horn, J. B. 58
Horn, Sarah 16
Horn, W. C. 29
Horn, William Cooper 16
Horn, William James 16,
  60
Horn family 58-60
Horne, Francis 14
Hornebeame Hall 57, 58
Horse and Groom
  alehouse 6, *12*, 24
horses 88
Horsehoes pub 42
Horsey, Edward William
  29, 34
Horsey, Fanny 30, 85

93

97

98

VICTOIRE MODES

ST. ALBANS

is time and money well spent —

A visit to-

OVER the years Hatfield Residents have availed themselves of our personal and complete family service.

97 VICTORIA STREET :

Lingerie, Wools and Knitwear.

109 VICTORIA STREET :

Ladies', Gent's and Children's selective footwear.

131 VICTORIA STREET :

Exclusive Children's Wear, Nursery Furniture and Prams.

133 VICTORIA STREET :

Ladies' Coats and Gowns. Elegant styles for Teenagers to Outsizes.

135 VICTORIA STREET :

Gent's and Boys' Outfitters. Leading makes in stock. Hertfordshire's largest School Outfitters.

H. W. WALBY & SON

HIGH-CLASS
BUTCHERS

The Broadway
Great North Road, Hatfield

Phone 2455

Printed in Great Britain
by Amazon

82562196R00037